# THE PATH OF ENLIGHTENMENT IN THE MITHRAIC MYSTERIES

JULIUS EVOLA

Translated, with an introduction,

by

GUIDO STUCCO

Department of Theology,

St. Louis University

*Foreword by The Evola Foundation*

*Rome, Italy*

THE ALEXANDRIAN PRESS

ISBN 1-55818-228-4

FOURTH EDITION,

REVISED

— 2011 —

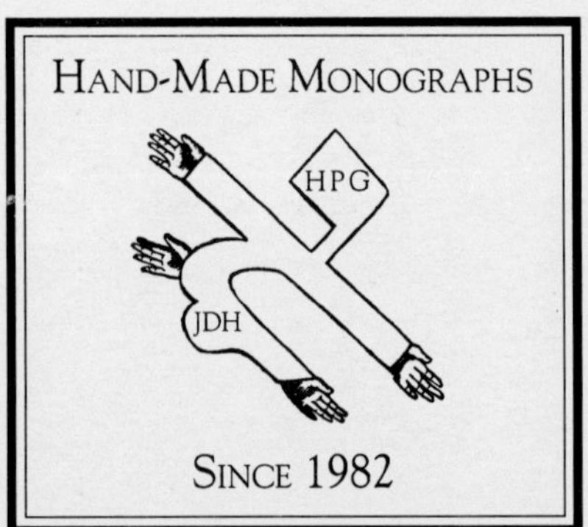


HOLMES PUBLISHING GROUP LLC
POSTAL BOX 2370
SEQUIM WA 98382 USA
JDHOLMES.COM

# FOREWORD
### The Julius Evola Foundation, Rome

The first and the third of the following essays written by Julius Evola are dedicated to the mysteries of Mithras, while the second essay concerns itself with the Roman Emperor, Julian. The first essay, published in the periodical *Ultra* (1926), describes some details of the initiation practiced in Mithraic mysteries. Mithras was the god of the heavenly light, warrantor of oaths, and the sworn enemy of all lies; his cult competed with Christianity for the spiritual primacy in the West, at a time when the Roman Empire had begun to decline.

The second essay by Evola was occasioned by the publication in 1932 of an Italian translation of some writings of Julian, and it was published again on March 17, 1972, with slight modifications, in the Italian daily newspaper *Roma*. Evola's work dealt with the noble figure of the Emperor, who was initiated in the cult of Mithras, as he attempted to revive the ancient sacred traditions.

In the third selection, which was first published during the 1950's and again in 1971 in the periodical *Vie della Tradizione*, Evola interpreted in great depth the various symbols which animated the myth of Mithras and which were present in the initiation ceremony.

The religious events of the Roman Empire still evoke the interest and the fascination of those who study the spiritual doctrines of the Ancients. The image of Mithras in the act of slaying the bull has been adopted by the Julius Evola Foundation as its emblem.

# Introduction

Who was Julius Evola? Considered by many a philosopher, others have cast him in the role of arch-reactionary. Regardless, his philosophical writings have earned him a place as one of the leading representatives of the Traditionalist school.

Like the American poet Ezra Pound before him, the term "fascist" has been accorded Evola for being among the opposition during WWII. For three decades he was shunned by the academic community which took little interest in his writings. Yet Evola has been the object of an interesting revival, acquiring a posthumous revenge of sorts. Conferences and *symposia* devoted to the analysis of his thought have "mushroomed" in the past fifteen years throughout Europe. Secondly, Evola has exercised a magical spell on many people who, having no interest in so-called progressive ideals, have taken a sharp turn toward Tradition in their quest for something "more transcendent" or for something of a "higher order." These new views cannot be readily found in the wasteland of contemporary society. Thirdly, his spiritual and metaphysical ideas, far from being an appendix to his *Weltanschauung*, represent its very core and can no longer be ignored. Evola's ideas call for a critical analysis and a reasonable response from sympathizers and critics alike.

The reader of these monographs will be able to find detailed information about Julius Evola's life and thought in Richard Drake's writings.[1] This introduction seeks to identify and to characterize the common themes running through all of the following treatises: — *The Path of the Enlightenment in the Mithraic Mysteries; Zen: The Religion of the Samurai; Taoism: The Magic, The Mysticism; Rene Guenon: A Teacher for Modern Times.* (Holmes Publishing Group, 1994.) Let us begin with the first theme.

Upon a cursory reading, it is immediately evident that Evola establishes a dichotomy between common, ordinary knowledge, and a secret knowledge which is the prerogative of a selected few. This distinction, also known to Plato, who distinguished between *doxa* and *episteme*, has been the legacy of the Mystery cults, of Mithraism, of Gnosticism, and of all initiatory chains, East or West.

The epistemological distinction between esoteric and exoteric knowledge is rooted, according to Evola, in the ontological classism which separates people, the multitudes, or the *oi polloi*, from the *aristoi*, the heroes, the kings, and the men of knowledge (priests and ascetics). One of the constants in Evola's thought, is his aversion for the empirical subject, who lives, eats, reproduces and dies; everything in his works represents a yearning for something which is more than ordinary existence, more than that condition of life which is heavily conditioned by routines, passions, cravings and superficiality, for what the Germans call *meher als leben* ("more than living"),—a sort of nostalgia for the *Hyperuranium*, for Transcendence, for "what was in the origins." Esotericism is the means to achieve the ultimate reality which all religions strive to achieve, though they call it by many names, as the late Joseph Campbell was fond of saying. During his career as a writer, Julius Evola was involved in an extensive, sophisticated study of esoteric doctrines. In these monographs we find Evola celebrating the metaphysical premises and techniques of Zen and of operative Taoism; elsewhere he sang the praise of Tantrism[2] and of early Buddhism.[3] In another work, commended by Carl Jung, he discussed Hermeticism.[4] Scholars of various disciplines will not forgive this controversial and brilliant Italian thinker his incursions in their own fields of competence, such as history, religion, mythology, and psychology. And yet Evola succeeds in weaving a colorful and suggestive pattern, which slowly and gracefully evolves into a well articulated, monolithic *Weltanschauung*.

Another distinctive feature of these works is Julius Evola's firm conviction in the existence of a hierarchy to which all states of being are subject. These states defy the imagination of ordinary people. In the Western religious tradition one does not easily find an articulated cosmology or for that matter a serious emphasis on the soul's experiences in its quest for God. There are the powerful exceptions represented by the writings of St. Bonaventure, St. John of the Cross, Jacob Boehme, St. Theresa of Avila, and other more obscure mystics.

Since the personal God of theism is believed to have brought the universe into being, Christianity's focus, in terms of cult and speculation, has shifted from the *cosmos* to its Creator. Evola's knowledge of the Christian tradition was not equal to the erudition he displayed in other subjects. Nevertheless, he attempted to fill what he considered a vacuum in the Christian system. In this monograph dedicated to Mithras he describes the states of being or the spiritual experiences of the initiate to Mithraic mystery tradition and wisdom. These Mithraic experiences are depicted as three-dimensional, heroic, cosmological and esoteric and are juxtaposed to the two-dimensional, devotional, liturgical and exoteric spiritual experiences of formal Christianity. In Evola's work on Zen he celebrates the hierarchical "five grades of merit," through which the initiate grows in wisdom and pursues the personal quest for enlightenment.

A third and final characteristic found in these selections is the rejection of theism and the polemics with Christianity, which in the piece on Guenon is merely outlined (see his comparison of the Christian and the initiatory views of immortality, found in the work on Taoism). His penetrating critique of theism was articulated in the name of "higher" principles and not by an *a priori* hostility to religion and to the concepts of supernatural authority and revelation. What he rejected in theism was the idea of faith, of devotion, of abandonment in a higher power. To faith he opposed experience; to devotion, heroic and ascetical action; to the God of theism, who is believed to be the ultimate reality, as well as the believer's goal and eschatological hope, Evola opposed the ideal of liberation and of enlightenment as you will find in this examination of Mithraism.

These monographs are a testimony to the restless curiosity and spiritual hunger of a nonspecialist who dared to venture into the domain of scholars and of specialized disciplines, only to extract precious gems of wisdom, unburdened by technical details and *minutiae* which are the obsession of scholars and of university professors. It is my sincere hope that interest in Julius Evola and his ideas will be generated by the translation of these monographs as they represent only a small portion of  many untranslated works which need to be brought to the attention of the English speaking world.

NOTES

1.  Richard Drake, "Julius Evola and the Ideological Origins of the Radical Right in Contemporary Italy," in *Political Violence and Terror: Motifs and Motivations*, ed., Peter Merkl (Berkeley: University of California Press, 1986), 61-89; "Julius Evola, Radical Fascism and the Lateran Accords," <u>The Catholic Historical Review</u> 74 (1988): 403-19; and "The Children of the Sun," chapter in *The Revolutionary Mystique and Terrorism in Contemporary Italy* (Bloomington: Indiana University Press, 1989).

2.  Julius Evola, *The Yoga of Power*, trans. Guido Stucco (Rochester, VT: Inner Traditions, 1992).

3.  Julius Evola, *The Doctrine of the Awakening*, trans. G. Mutton (London: Luzac Co, 1951).

4.  Julius Evola, *The Hermetic Tradition*, trans. E. Rhemus (Rochester, VT: Inner Traditions, 1993).

THE PATH OF ENLIGHTENMENT ACCORDING
TO THE MYSTERIES OF MITHRAS

At a particular level of spiritual development it is immediately evident
that the myths of the Mystery religions are essentially an allegory of the states of
consciousness which are experienced by the initiate on the path toward self-
realization. The various deeds and adventures of mythical heroes are not poetical,
but *real* events; they are the specific actions of one's inner being and shine forth
from within the one who attempts to follow the path of initiation which leads
beyond the fulfillment of the merely human mode of existence. These adventures
are not allegorical concepts, but experiences. The philosophico-allegorical
interpretation of myths is still mere allegory and no less superficial than the
naturalistic and anthropomorphic interpretation of myths. This implies that
people can learn a valuable lesson from this subject only if they already *know*
something; otherwise the "door" remains inexorably shut. This also applies to
what I am going to say about the inner meaning of the Mithras myth.[1]

The Mithraic mysteries lead to the very heart of the magical Western
tradition—a world characterized by self- affirmation, light, greatness, regal
spirituality and spiritual regality. In this path there is no room for escapism; or
asceticism; or mortification of the self through humility and devotion; or
renunciation and contemplative abstraction. Mithras' path is one of action, of
solar power and of spirituality, which is opposed to both the dull and dreamy
oriental universalism[2] and to Christian sentimentalism and moralism.

It is said that only a "man" could proceed along this path; any "woman"
would be consumed and broken by the "taurine strength." The brightness of
the *hvareno*, of the glorious and radiant Mithraic halo, arises only out of a
frightful tension, and it only crowns the "eagle," which was capable of "staring"
at the Sun.

Mithras is the symbol of those who proceed along this path. In the myth he
is thought to be the primordial heavenly light which manifests itself as a "god
generated from a rock" (*theos ek petras, to petroghenos Mithra*). While standing
on the bank of a river, he frees himself, escaping the obscure mineral by wielding
the sword and torch which helped him while he was in the "mother's" womb.
This is a miraculous birth, noticed only by "shepherds" hidden on the
"mountaintops."

What I have mentioned so far is a body of symbols related to what may be
called the initiation phase in the strict sense of the word. The heavenly "light,"

which was the light of the Word, but men could not comprehend (Jn 1:9.10), is rekindled in he who experiences his first spiritual birth. This birth occurs when one breaks away from the "god of this earth" and is able to withstand the onslaught of the *waters*. This light is rejected by the principle which informs ordinary people's lives and the *stuff* on which their ephemeral being, their lights and certainties are based. This principle is characterized by a frenzied, shallow and confused activity; by a blind race toward the "abyss"; by a deep-seated greed which perpetuates, through the chain of rebirths, (that is, through different lives sharing the same inconsistency and transience), an hetero-centric life-style, characterized by an insatiable craving for various things.

This wild and unrestrained vital force, which first generates and then devours its own energies in a context of radical contingency,[3] corresponds to the symbol of the "waters" at the edge of which Mithras is generated. An initiate is one who is "rescued from the waters" (notice the connection with the Moses legend as recounted in *Exodus*), and who "walks on water" (hence the esoteric meaning of Christ's miracle). The initiate is a being who has learned how to take control of the *totality* of the cravings and the deficiencies which urge him internally. He has learned how to resist them, and has the power to say NO, and how to break their law and how to develop a new life without them. On the contrary, the beings of the "sub-lunar world"[4] continue to experience death, annihilation, or reabsorption.

Thus, to be initiated is like leaving behind a bank of a river, on which people's lives unfold with all their miseries and greatness. At that point one has to face the current which becomes increasingly furious until he reaches the middle of the "river";[5] then he has to move beyond this limitation and to struggle toward the opposite bank. Once the opposite bank has been attained, a new, spiritual being is born: Mithras, the Divine Child.

The "rock" which acts as the womb of Mithras, is a symbol of the body. The body is the substratum of cosmic yearning, and the element which is subjected to the "wet principle." Thus the *waters* also dominate all those human states and faculties, whether "spiritual" or not, which exist in a physical substratum. In order to become initiated one has to become free from the "rock" and to achieve a state of consciousness which is no longer limited by the connection with the bodily vehicle. Likewise, the following episodes which I am going to refer to, are out-of-body experiences which take place in a special state induced by specific practices, which I am not going to describe in detail.

The expression "*theos ek petras*" carries yet another meaning in the magical tradition. On the one hand, the precipitation of what constitutes the "heavenly light" into the dungeon represented by the dark "earth," is a negative and degenerative process; but, on the other hand, it also represents an opportunity for the spiritual element to become individuated and actualized. The body's sophisticated organism witnesses the presence of a nucleus of qualified energy. Magical initiation does not consist in dissolving such a nucleus into the indistinct fluctuation of cosmic life. On the contrary, it consists in strengthening and integrating it. Thus, an initiation consists in carrying this nucleus *forward*, not backwards. According to initiatory thought, the spirit is not "something else," but rather something immanent, which needs to be elevated from the pits of concrete human reality (the "rock"). This reality is divine, not by grace, but according to its own nature; hence the expression "generative rock" (the equivalent concept in the Hermetic-Alchemical tradition is that of the "material required in the *Opus Magnum*") and the attribute of *petrogenos* (generated from the rock) which is bestowed on the Man-god, Mithras, who does not descend from Heaven, but who is derived from the Earth.

The "nakedness" of the divine child finds its complementary symbols in the notions of "being rescued from the waters"; of "being extracted from the rock"; of "throwing away the clothes" and of "being washed." These symbols are found in many esoteric traditions. To be "naked" is the equivalent of being pure, which in this context refers to autarchy, self-sufficiency, detachment from anything and anybody.

With particular reference to the will, esoteric traditions call a will *impure* when it is pre-occupied and determined by various factors, such as objects, purposes, reasons, or passions. It is also called *impure* because a will such as this is unable to proceed by itself, to want and to assert itself, or to resolve itself in a pure form. In the West, this pure form (which the Hindu call *nishakama-karma* as opposed to *sakama-karma*, which is an action willed for the sake of the results it will yield), is symbolized by the "Virgin." This "Virgin" tramples under her feet the "Snake" and the "Moon" (two symbols for the *waters*), and through a "virginal conception," she gives birth to the divine child. The so-called *autozoon*, which is a self-generated life subsisting beyond the contingency of human nature, springs from a "virginal" and purified will which is free of all bonds, consisting only of pure act. In the Mithraic ritual, mention is made of "the existence of the soul's power in a state of uncontaminated purity"; this existence generates a new nucleus beyond the *waters*. This nucleus, in turn, once it develops into a new being, goes on to populate a world which is beyond the human dimension, beyond space and time.

Such a miraculous birth is perceived only by "shepherds hidden in the Mountain." The symbol of the Mountain refers to those superior spiritual beings who command and who direct in an invisible way the great currents of the *waters*. The *waters* symbolize the historical and social forces, the traditions, the beliefs and the collective psychic system which dominate the passive beings who, living like a flock, inhabit the sublunar world. The Mountain itself is symbolic of a particular state of metaphysical consciousness, which is echoed in the "Sermons on the Mount" which are found in various traditions.

But in order to attain virility, the new being must undergo new and more difficult trials, in which he can experience either victory or catastrophe. Since Mithras is superior to the world inhabited by inferior natures, he must also achieve superiority over the world of those spiritual natures which his out-of-body condition progressively discloses to him.

The myth goes on to say that once Mithras is beyond the *waters*, a "furious wind invests and scourges his naked body, as he feels the presence of terrible powers arising all around him." Without hesitation, Mithras approaches a *tree*, and proceeds to pluck and to eat of its fruit. From the leaves he fashions a "garment." Now he is ready to contend with the lords of the wonderful world in which he has entered.

This refers to a series of particular states of consciousness, which are attracted to "nakedness," or to the element of the will in its purest and most free state. The "wind" alludes to an experience which is very characteristic and yet difficult to communicate. I will try to explain it with an example. To say "I love," or "I hate," is to presume an imaginary property. Feelings, in their essence, are universal, cosmic realities which become actualized in various beings, in the same way fire is produced whenever the mechanisms leading up to combustion are present. One should not say: "I love," but rather: "Love loves in me." What is commonly called "personality," is actually nothing more than the result of the dynamic interaction of such impersonal forces; thus "personality" lacks a true existence in itself, and it cannot attribute such forces to itself.

When this aggregate is dissolved[6] by the *ignis essentiae* (the fire of initiation as well as the blaze of death[7]), something continues to exist, such as an identity of consciousness, which in the Alchemical tradition is called "golden, incorruptible grain." The above mentioned forces, once freed from the phenomenal, particular and psychological world in which they are experienced by mankind, manifest themselves to this something in their true nature, as cosmic forces. But *vis a vis* these forces one is as impotent as a physical being confronted by the fury of the elements of nature, such as oceans, thunderbolts and cataclysms. In his nakedness the initiate is animated by these forces. When the "waves" created by these forces push him to the deepest dimensions of his inner being, the initiate cannot do anything but remain still and non-reacting, lest he be swept away. According to the hermetic work *Tabula smaragdina*, or The Emerald Tablet, these waves constitute the "wind" which carries the *Thelesma*, which is the principle destined to draw to itself the power of all things, whether they be of a higher or of a lower nature.

This trial, which some esoteric Christian traditions hide behind the symbol of "flagellation," bestows on Mithras a firmness and an unbreakable nature, without which he would lose his life in the trial which follows.

This trial requires nothing short of a complete turnabout, this time in the affirmative sense of the word, opposite to what the Biblical myth refers to as original sin. The Self dares to do violence to the "Tree of Life," to defoliate it and to eat its fruits. The Self is strong enough to snatch away from the Universal Principle a certain amount of cosmic power and to dominate it, meaning that it has the capability to stand up against the "water" and the "wind." This is performing a radical deed, an absolute action and going beyond oneself. This action creates a vacuum, immediately filled by a force which envelops, in the form of a flame, the naked nature responsible for such a daring feat. In many traditions, this deed is referred to as the "projection of fire," an eminently positive act which attracts a negative element; it has also been called a "feminine descent,"[8] which becomes the nucleus' *garment of power*. Dressed with this garment, the newly constituted nucleus acquires the means to manifest and to project itself, which is as necessary for life in the super-sensory dimension, as the physical vehicle is necessary in the sensory life.

Thus, the power which becomes precipitated is in need of a center and those who, after having evoked this power, do not know how to provide it with a center, are swept away by it. The "Fall" refers precisely to this. The "fall" consists in failing in the course of this action, or in "the Kingdom of Heaven, or Fate, suffering violence"; or in one assuming Life in its entirety; or in being overwhelmed by a terror which immediately sweeps away and destroys an individual.[9] The latter is a possible catastrophic outcome. Others, on the contrary, prove to be sufficient to their own act. They can break the curse, take upon themselves the power, retain it and dominate it. Far from "falling," they are "reborn in power," in the "mighty strength of all strengths," in the "incorruptible Right Hand." Mithras is one of these people; not only does he not submit to the law, but he draws from his action the strength necessary to turn *against* the One who upholds the law and, in turn, to subject him to his own law.

Here the peculiar character of magical initiations is apparent. Actually, there is a tendency, in a number of schools of thought which should be regarded as mystical rather than esoteric, to dissolve the individual in an impersonal reality,[10] whether it is described as the undifferentiated infinite (e.g., the *nirguna-brahman* of the Vedantic tradition) or as a transcendent order or harmony. To dissolve the Self's nucleus in this impersonal reality, "as a grain of salt is dissolved in an ocean of water," is the declared goal of these schools of thought, which view any notion of affirmation, struggle and spiritual subordination as utterly meaningless. Conversely, the Magical Tradition understands the spiritual world in very different terms, inasmuch as it firmly upholds the notion of individual, or that of an affirmative center existing beyond any "dissolution," although in other terms than merely physical and personal ones. The Magical Tradition does not view the spiritual world as characterized by an idyllic order or by an undifferentiated universality, but rather as an ensemble of unrestrained, abyssal forces existing in a state which is free, terrible and blissful at the same time. These forces are thought to be caught in an interplay of tensions, compared to which, anything which human beings call "struggle" is only a pale and cadaverous reflex. Each one of these entities continues to exist and to retain its individuality in the same proportion in which it has the ability to withstand and resist other entities which, in turn, are trying to attract and to assimilate it. This is a world existing in a free state, not governed by any providential plan, nor subject to any teleological and aprioristic ordering law to which the various forces are simply supposed to conform. The only real *a priori* are these very forces. All the laws and systems are nothing more than the by-products of the organization of these forces, and nothing more than the signs of a wider power which has succeeded in sweeping away, assuming and unifying other powers underneath it, thus decreasing the primordial chaos of the various struggling forces.

In this context, the struggle is very different from the struggle which usually takes place in the material world. Destructive violence, hatred, will power, strength in the physical sense of the word, are not found in this world. What takes place is more a confrontation of "presences," an encounter between different degrees of being and between diverse quantities of spiritual intensity. No power *wants*, strictly speaking, to overcome and to dominate others. However, this takes place naturally, as a consequence of a higher degree of being. This higher degree of being acts upon lower powers as a deep vortex, which swallows and dominates them whenever they come in contact with it. In this context, in order to come out victorious, namely to retain one's autonomy, the secret is to *endure*. Any force which invests a being without succeeding in sweeping it away, is in turn swept away and subjugated by that being. There is no gap, no safe area in this world of tensions where not to subordinate means to become subordinated.

Hence the saying, which is a law to those who are called *masters*: "Do not reveal yourself to others." This concept gave J.G. Frazer the subject matter for his main work, about the priest of the mysteries (the "King of the Woods") and his dignity, which was confirmed only by triumphing over a challenger. Hence, the strange saying according to which a student who succeeds, *kills* his teacher; and, finally, hence the puzzling Eastern notion according to which the "gods" are enemies of the *yogin*. In the "lunar" path, or the path of Isis, what matters is to turn oneself into an obedient instrument of higher entities. In the magic, "solar" path, or path of *Ammon*, the most important action is to retain one's being *vis a vis* these entities; this, however, is not possible other than by overcoming them. One must wrestle away from them the "quantity" of fate which they carry, in order to take upon oneself their weight and responsibility.

When Mithras reaches this point, "doors" are thrown open and around him shines the light of "those who are"—terrible powers who stare at the newcomer. Beyond them all is the Sun, the flaming *Æon*. In this terrible instant, which creates a barren silence, the desert, the terror of great catastrophes and of great sacrileges, Mithras endures and stares at the great god. He ceases his prayers and commands. And lo, the god yields and asks Mithras to confer the initiation on him and to sign a pact of mutual respect and friendship.

This climax marks the end of the first great phase of initiation: a being has come into existence, stronger than nature, stronger than the gods—a being who is beyond birth and death.

I have previously mentioned that the experiences Mithras underwent correspond to a series of spiritual realizations taking place immediately and directly outside the body. In the case of the initiate, this is supposed to happen through the induction of particular states of consciousness. He who induces these states is a qualified person (the *hierophant*, in the Mysteries); these states constitute both a problem and a trial which the initiate must resolve through a determinate act of his spiritual being. But in the Mithraic mysteries, there is a further realization, which corresponds to the myth of the "slaying of the bull."

The task consists in this: to reaffirm the solar and royal apex, which is realized outside the physical realm, in the body itself, in the dark "rock" which had been left behind during this entire phase. Mithras now has to grapple with and eventually subjugate the wild and untamed power of life, symbolized by the "bull." This deed involves disciplines which affect the body itself, and which tend to alter in a radical way the relationship which the body has with the Self. This is not the place to discuss the methods employed for this purpose; it suffices to say that these methods range from the exclusive assumption of the "fire" of mental concentration, to the adequate employment of psychic traumas such as those encountered in suffering or during sexual excitement. The Hindu schools focus mainly on disciplines which are related to breathing. Since the ritual described by Dieterich shows how they are also employed in Mithraic theurgy, I will briefly mention them. A word of caution is due, since these practices are either useless or extremely dangerous to those who have not yet made the experiences I have described so far.

Mithras grasps the "bull," holding onto his horns. He jumps on its back and rides it. The beast breaks into a gallop and takes its rider for a wild and dangerous ride. Mithras holds firm, and lets himself "be carried," hanging from the horns. The bull soon becomes exhausted and returns to the "cave" whence it came out. Mithras holds him "still," and then finishes the beast off with a dagger, in the name of the Sun.

I have already mentioned that the "bull" symbolizes the elementary life-force. It is to be identified with the *Green Dragon* of Alchemy, with tantric *kundalini* or with the Taoist "Dragon." The disciplines which focus on breathing call this force *prana*—a breathing considered in its "luminous" and "subtle" dimension. *Prana* is related to material breathing as the soul is to the body. This life-force is naturally evasive and resists coercion; it is the restless "mercury," the "volatile," the "bird" (the *hamsah* bird of the Hindu tradition, *ham* and *sah* being respectively the sound of inhaling and exhaling), which the initiate has to "ride" and to "immobilize." The practice consists in focused breathing and in becoming lost in it; then, boldly, in letting go, in sinking. This is what the expression "the Dragon flies away" is supposed to mean.

According to the initiatory disciplines found in Hinduism, breath has four dimensions: a material dimension (*sthula*), related to the state of wakefulness and to the cerebral-psychological faculties; a subtle, luminous dimension (*sukshma*), related to the dream state and to the nervous system; a causative, igneous dimension (*karana*), related to the state of deep sleep and to the blood system; and finally a dimension which the Hindu texts call *turiya* (the fourth), which is related to the special state observed in catalepsy: a state of apparent death, related to the skeleton and the reproductive function.

Mithras, who after taking hold of the bull "lets himself be carried" in a wild ride without ever letting go, symbolizes the Self which, as it sinks, goes through these four stages and through the neutral areas separating them. By contrast, ordinary people simply lose consciousness and fall asleep at the very first stage. The bull gives up only when Mithras shows enough boldness and a subtle enduring strength, or until the process of "sinking" reaches the fourth stage.[11] At this point, the basic mechanisms of the primitive life-force are seized and brought to a halt; the *mercury* is fixed and congealed; the "bull" is *slain*. The life-force, finally deprived of all support, is suspended, broken, burnt to the roots.

Once this climactic point is reached a miraculous transformation occurs. A blazing, whirling, divine life arises from the deep, quick as lightning. This new life-force permeates the whole body with a gleaming which transfigures it. It re-creates the body *ab imo*, as an entity of pure activity, as a glorious body of immortal splendor; this is the "radiating body," the *augoeides*, the *Hvareno*, the *vajra*, the *Dorje*. These are all different names recurring in various Eastern and Western traditions, describing the same force. This new life-force, which has the nature of diamond and of irresistible thunderbolt, transforms the mortal and deprived condition into one of immortality.

What oozes from the bull's wound is not blood, but wheat, the Bread of Life, as a perennial source created by the surrounding desert and as the miracle of a new kind of vegetation. However one obstacle still needs to be overcome: swarms of impure animals crowd around the dying bull to drink its blood and to bite its genitals, thus poisoning the source of life. This is the last episode in this saga; the meaning of this is that the prodigious and superhuman power, called *kundalini* in Hindu tradition, is awakened once the bull is slain. This power immediately floods all the principles and the functions which support the physical being. If during this process all these elements have not been purified, organized and unified, they become unleashed, absorbing and transforming to their advantage the higher power which was supposed to transform them into a *spiritual body*. What ensues, therefore, is a terrible setback, an emanation, a gushing forward of those forces which belong to the animal and emotive nature, and which are now extraordinarily excited. This phenomenon has been variously called the "clouding of the sky," "the storm," or the "deluge." In the alchemical and Taoist traditions, this "storm" is said to occur after somebody has drunk the "Virgin's milk," which is the "Dragon's blood." In the myth of Mithras this phenomenon corresponds to the swarming of the impure animals.

It is unlikely that this experience could be entirely avoided, since it is the very last trial. But lo, after it has taken place, the sky opens up and the miracle continues. The last obscure obstacles are swept away by the rising flood of light and sound, illuminating what is latent, obscure, buried, contracted in the form of bodily organs, in gestures, in a powerful and cosmic enlightenment. This constitutes the ascent of the man-god to the heavenly spheres, to the hierarchy of the "seven planets." Here the external dimension of things fades away, becomes inwardly bright, and then *burns up*. Everything becomes alive, awakens and is reborn from within; everything becomes symbolic, meaningful, radiant—the spirit of an unlimited and eternal body.

Beyond the seventh sphere lies the ULTIMATE, where there no longer is a "here" or a "there," but calmness, enlightenment and solitude as an infinite ocean. It is the dimension of the "Father," beyond which lies the dimension of the "Eagle," the apex, the substratum of the flaming, whirling world of powers.

This is the path and the challenge open to man, according to Mithraic wisdom, which competed with Christianity to inherit the legacy of the Roman empire. Once it was pushed back and relegated to the external, exoteric plane, the efficiency of the mystery wisdom was preserved in the occult tradition, but it continued to operate on Western historical events, exercising a subtle, invisible influence. Today, once again, it surfaces again beyond that world which science has "liberated" and which philosophy has "internalized." It re-emerges in attempts still very confused; in beings who have been broken under the weight of a truth too heavy for them, which however others will know how to take up and to affirm. It re-emerges in Nietzsche, in Weininger, in Braum, in the most radical trajectories of the most recent Idealism. It re-emerges in myself, in my yearning for the infinite, in the only value that I cherish: a regal and solar life, a life of light, freedom and power.

It is encouraging to come across scholarly works which go beyond the prejudices and the distortions characterizing most viewpoints of contemporary historians. This is the case of Raffaello Prati, who has translated into Italian and introduced to the general public the Roman Emperor Julian Flavius' speculative writings, collectively entitled *"On Gods and Men."*

It is noteworthy that Prati employed the term "Emperor Julian" instead of the prevalent expression "Julian the Apostate." As a matter of fact, the term "apostate" is hardly suitable since it should rather be applied to those who abandoned the sacred traditions and cults which were the very soul of ancient Rome's greatness and who accepted a new faith, which was not of Roman or Latin stock, but of Asiatic and Jewish origin. Thus, the term "apostate" should not characterize those who, like Julian Flavius, dared to be faithful to the spirit of Tradition and who attempted to reaffirm the solar and sacred ideal of the Empire.

The reading of the newly published texts, which were written by Julian in his tent, between long marches and battles (as if to draw from his spirit new energies in order to face difficult events), should also benefit those who follow the current opinion which defines paganism, in its religious components, as more or less synonymous with superstition. In fact, Julian, in his attempt to restore Tradition, opposed to Christianity a metaphysical vision. Julian's writings allow us to see, behind the allegorical and external elements of pagan myths, a substance of higher quality.

Julian made a very important point when he wrote:

> Whenever myths on sacred subjects are incongruous in thought, by that very fact they cry aloud, as it were, and summon us not to believe them literally, but to study and track down their hidden meaning.... When the meaning is expressed incongruous there is some hope that men will neglect the more obvious sense of the words, and that pure intelligence may rise to the comprehension of the distinctive nature of the gods that transcends all existing things.[12]

This should be the hermeneutical principle employed by those who study ancient mythologies and theologies. Thus, when scholars use disparaging terms such as "superstition" or "idolatry," they prove to be closed-minded and in bad faith.

Therefore, in the re-evaluation of the ancient sacred Roman tradition, attempted by Julian, it is the esoteric view of the nature of the "gods" and their "knowledge," that ultimately matters. This knowledge corresponds to an inner realization. In this perspective the gods are not portrayed as poetic inventions or as abstractions of philosophizing theologians, but rather as the symbols and the projections of transcendent states of consciousness.

Thus, Julian himself, as an initiate to Mithras' mysteries, saw a close connection between a superior knowledge of one's self and the path which leads to the "knowledge of the gods"; the latter is such a noble goal that he did not shun from saying that dominion over Roman and barbarian lands pales in comparison.

This brings us back to the tradition of a secret discipline through which the knowledge of one's self is radically transformed and strengthened by new powers and inner states, which are symbolized in ancient theology by the various *numina*. This transformation is said to occur after an initial preparation, consisting in living a pure life and in practicing asceticism and eventually in undergoing special experiences which are determined by initiatory rites.

*Helios* was the power to which Julian dedicated his hymn, whose name he invoked even in his dying words, while dying at sunset on a battlefield in Asia Minor. *Helios* is the sun, which is not conceived as a deified physical body, but rather as a symbol of metaphysical light and transcendent power. This power manifests itself in mankind and in those who have been regenerated, as a sovereign *nous* and as a mystical force from above. In ancient days and even in Rome itself, via Persian influence, this force was considered to be strictly associated with the royal dignity. The true meaning of the imperial Roman cult which Julian attempted to restore and to institutionalize over and against Christianity, can be appreciated only in this context. The central *motif* in this cult is: the true and legitimate leader is the only one who is endowed with a supernatural ontological superiority and who is an image of the king of heaven, namely *Helios* himself. When this occurs (and only then), authority and hierarchy are justified; the *regnum* is sanctified; and a luminous center of gravity is to be found, which draws to itself a number of human and natural forces.

Julian yearned to implement this "pagan" ideal within a stable and unitary imperial hierarchy, endowed with a dogmatic foundation, a system of disciplines and laws, and a priestly class. The priestly class was supposed to have as its leader the emperor himself who, having been regenerated and elevated above the mere mortal condition by the Mysteries, embodied simultaneously spiritual authority and temporal power. According to this view, the emperor was believed to be the *Pontifex Maximus*, an ancient term restored by Augustus. The ideological presuppositions on which Julian's vision rested, were: *I.*) nature, believed to form an harmonious whole and to be permeated by living but invisible forces; *II.*) a State professed monotheism; *III.*) a body of "philosophers" (it would be better to call them *wise men*) capable of interpreting the traditional theology of ancient Rome and of actualizing it through initiatory rites.

This view is in stark contrast with early Christianity's dualism, exemplified by Jesus' saying "render unto Caesar what is Caesar's and unto God what is

God's." This saying eventually led Christians to refuse to pay homage to the emperor in any other role than as a ruler. This refusal, incidentally, was considered to be a political display of anarchy and of subversion, and it culminated in the State's persecutions against the Christians.

Unfortunately the times were not ripe for the implementation of Julian's ideal. Such an implementation would have required active participation of, and synergy between, all the social *strata* of society as well as a recasting of the ancient *Weltanschauung* in more vibrant terms. Instead, an irreversible separation between form and content took place within pagan society.

Even the consensus which Christianity had obtained was a fatal sign of the decadence of the times. To the vast majority of people, to talk about the gods as inner experiences or to consider the above mentioned transcendent and solar principles as necessary requirements to the empire was nothing else but a fiction or a mere "philosophy." In other words, what was lacking was an *existential* foundation. Besides, Julian deluded himself into thinking he would be able to transform certain esoteric teachings into formative political, cultural and social forces. These teachings, due to their very nature, were destined, however, to fall within the competency of only restricted circles.

This should not make us conclude that, at least in principle, a contradiction existed between Julian's vision and the ideal of a state-enforced application of those spiritual and transcendent elements. The mere historical existence of a succession of civilizations which were centered on a "solar" spirituality (spanning from ancient Egypt and ancient Iran, to Japan prior to World War II) should demonstrate that such a contradiction does not really exist. It should rather be said that Rome, during Julian's time, lacked the human and spiritual substance capable of establishing connections and relationships of participation which characterize a new living hierarchy as a totalitarian imperial organism worthy of the name pagan.

The celebrated text by Dmitri Merezhkovsky, *Death of the Gods*, captures in an admirable and suggestive way the cultural climate of Julian's times, with its forebodings of a *twilight of the gods*.

Following a long parenthesis, some elements of the ancient Tradition were destined to resurface when, thanks to the emergence of the Germanic dynasties on the scenes of European history, it became possible to speak again of *restauratio imperii*, in the form of the medieval Sacred Roman Empire. This is true especially if we consider the Ghibelline tradition which attempted to reclaim for the Empire, against the hegemonical demands of the Church, a supernatural dignity not inferior to that which the Church herself enjoyed.

In regard to this, it is important to closely examine what was hidden in the chivalrous literature, in the so-called imperial *legend* and in other documents as well. I have attempted to gather and to adequately interpret all these sources in my book *Il mistero del graal e la tradizione ghibellina dell'impero* (1937).[13]

E. Renan once wrote: "If Christianity had succumbed to some deadly 'disease', the world would have become *Mithracized*." In other words, it would have adopted the religion of Mithras. According to a common opinion shared by many scholars Mithraism was the strongest and most enticing rival Christianity ever encountered. Mithraism arrived in Rome during the first half of the first century B.C. and reached its *apogee* around the third century A.D. Eventually, the religion spread to the ends of the empire, where for the most part, it attracted former legionnaires who had become farmers. Mithraism was congenial to their virile and fighting spirit and such emperors as Hadrian, Commodus and Aurelianus were initiated in its mysteries.

At the end of the second century A.D., Mithraism was officially acknowledged as the religion of the Empire with Mithras considered its patron-saint and champion. Mithras' cult had also merged with the cult of the Sun-God *Helios*, who was regarded as sovereign and invincible divine power. On December 25, the date of winter solstice (*die natalis Solis invicti Mithra*), the sun's rising again was celebrated as one of the most important Mithraic feast days. In their subverting work, Christians adopted this holiday, and turned it into Christmas. It is believed that Constantine hesitated between Christianity and Mithraism, while Julian became a famous initiate to these mysteries. This emperor employed Mithraism, as well as neo-Platonic metaphysics and mystery traditions, in his bold and noble attempt to restore the Roman pagan cults to counter the rapid spread of the Christian faith.

I have my reservations about the possibility that the ancient world might have become *Mithracized* instead of Christianized. In order to successfully compete with Christianity, Mithraism would have had to lower its own standards. Even if it had remained unadulterated, it is very unlikely that it would have won the same popular support enjoyed by the religion of Jesus, which was characterized by a sentimental doctrine of salvation open to all who sought it. Mithraism was a branch of an ancient Persian religion called Mazdeism. It was from Mazdeism that the cult of Mithras derived its central *motif* of a struggle between the forces of light/good and the forces of darkness/evil. Mithraism may have had religious and exoteric forms, but its central nucleus was found in its mysteries, namely in an initiation, in the true sense of the word. This separation between religion and initiation, which later became increasingly accentuated, was *per se* a limitation of Mithraism, though it made of Mithraism a more complete form of Tradition.

At this point I would like to focus on the Mithraic mysteries, and to characterize their nature on the basis of testimonies gathered from ancient writers or from scenes depicted on various ancient monuments found in the same areas of the centers of that cult and its mysteries. Besides these testimonies, which were gathered by Franz Cumont in one of his main works, I will discuss the *"Mithraic Ritual of the Great Magical Papyrus,"* (*Apathanatismos* in Greek), which is now kept in Paris. This text, with a translation and a commentary, can be found in the first volume of the work, *Introduzione alla Magia*.

I believe it is important to analyze and seek the inner meaning of the Mithras myth, beginning with the various episodes portrayed in ancient sculptures and *bas-reliefs*, some of which are of an exquisite workmanship. It is noteworthy to remember that such myths were a dramatization of the very experiences which the person to be initiated had to undergo. The drama was a repetition of the feats of the god with whom the initiate was supposed to identify.

According to the myth, Mithras is born or generated from a rock lying near a "river" (*theos ek petras, petrogenos Mithra*) as a manifestation of the primordial Uranic light; this miraculous birth is only noticed by the "guardians" hidden on the mountaintops nearby. As far as these "guardians" are concerned, they may be referred to as "Invisible Masters," and related to those primordial beings who, according to Hesiod, never died but who continue to live in the following ages and who can be called, "Those who are awake."

The "waters" and the "rock" may refer to the dualism of the stream of becoming and the principle which dominates it. The *rock* appears in many traditions with numerous significations. It is tempting to establish an analogy between Mithras' birth and one of the elements found in the Arthurian saga, namely a sword fixed in stone which floats on the water. When rising from the stone, Mithras holds with one hand a sword and with the other hand a torch, both symbols of strength (the former) and of enlightening power (the latter).

The rock may also be understood as a symbol of inner strength and steadiness, which are qualities required of the person to be initiated. These necessary qualities will constitute the foundation of his rebirth.

According to what we gather from the ancients, and especially from Nonnus the Grammarian, the neophytes of the Mithraic mysteries were required to undergo trials such as passing through fire and water and showing their endurance to cold, hunger and thirst. According to some other sources, the neophyte was involved in a simulated slaying of another person, in order to test his impassibility and resolve.

It may well be that such a qualification is related to the symbol of the *generative rock*, which is one of the requirements of an initiatory rebirth. In any event, the above mentioned qualities were required in later developments of Mithras' myth, since the latter had to withstand a strong wind which invested and scourged his naked body. Then Mithras proceeds straight to a tree and clothes himself with its leaves and feeds on its fruits. Considering the initiatory meaning of the tree, we may identify it with the tree which Adam yearned to touch in order to "become like one of us" (a god); however in the book of *Genesis* the access to the tree is precluded to him by the Old Testament's *Jehova*.

This interpretation may be supported by a further episode in this saga, concerning a confrontation between Mithras and the Sun, the flaming *Æon*. This episode ends with a pact between them. After this, Mithras becomes the bearer of the sovereign power of the Sun. This power corresponds to the *hvareno*, or the Glory, of the ancient Mazdean (Persian) tradition. This Glory was pictured as a supernatural fire engulfing heavenly deities—a fire which sometimes descended upon kings to enlighten, to consecrate and to grant them victory. The ontological status of a king upon whom this "glory" descended was believed to soar above that of his fellow human beings and he was considered to be immortal by his subjects. After Mithras had been identified with the Sun, who always triumphs over darkness, he became the protector and the chief deity of the Roman empire.

Mithras' dignity is also related to the focal episode of his saga, namely the slaying of the bull. Mithras spies the bull and waits. As soon as the bull emerges from a cave, he jumps on its back and rides the beast while holding onto the horns. The bull breaks into a gallop, dragging Mithras along in a mad rush. Mithras does not let go and lets himself be carried along without allowing the animal to throw him down, until the bull returns to its cave where Mithras finally slays it with his sword.

This is a representation of the struggle between the elemental and "infernal" life-force and its transformation by the one who has taken control of and will eventually overcome it. The blood which oozes out of the bull is turned into "spikes of wheat." As they touch the ground, the drops produce "vegetation." It is however necessary to prevent impure animals (often portrayed in the depictions of the myth) from drinking that blood. This also has an esoteric meaning; if the initiate, or the hero, is not "pure," those elements of an inferior nature which are still left in him would be strengthened by the energy which has been unleashed. Not only would this abort the transfiguration, but the final outcome may turn out to be disastrous and dangerous (this danger has been pointed out also in alchemical Hermeticism, though through a different symbolism). According to another version of the myth, the bull's blood is transformed into wine. This may refer to some of the effects induced by magical intoxication.

This episode in the myth became so important that it developed into a specific ritual in the initiation ceremonies: a baptism of blood. The *mitrei*, namely those places in which the mysteries were celebrated, were built in such a way to include both a higher and a lower part and usually in the form of an underground passages. The neophyte who passed the preliminary tests was placed in the lower passages; while standing naked, he was smeared with the blood of a bull slain by the *hierophant*, which dripped down from higher quarters. Other similar experiences must also have been associated with such a baptism of blood, the equivalent of the Christian baptismal rite.

As far as the experiences of somebody initiated into the Mithraic mysteries are concerned, a note should be made of the aforementioned ritual, called *apothanatismos*. In this ritual one will find Mithraic elements mingled with elements derived from Gnosticism and from other magical traditions. Dieterich, who was the first to publish a translation of this suggestive text (1903), called it a "liturgy." This characterization is not accurate, since this is not a ceremony filled with hymns or things of that sort, but rather a ritual filled with instructions, magical formulæ and invocations, as well as with an outline of corresponding experiences. The ritual seems to presuppose a preliminary initiation, since the person, in the course of his first invocation, claims to have been purified by "sacred ceremonies" and to have been empowered by the "mighty strength of all strengths" and by the "incorruptible Right Hand." Now he could aspire to the "immortal birth," elude the law of Fate which rules over the lower worlds, and contemplate the gods and the Æon, who is the "Lord of the fiery halos." The ritual relates how doors burst open, disclosing Seven Beings, who are first seen in their feminine aspect, and later in their masculine aspect as "Lords of the Heavenly Pole." The theurgic action leads one beyond the Seven Beings, until, in the midst of thunderbolts and flashes of dazzling lights, a figure appears: it is the Sun-Mithras himself, whom the *miste* must learn to stare at. Finally, at a command, one must vow never to depart from him again, and thus become transformed into Him (in order to assume his nature), to the point of "dying, having been integrated in the *palingenesis*, and reaching fulfillment in this very integration."

The ritual includes several other details, which I will not discuss in this context. The reader can refer to the text, which, as I have mentioned, has been translated from Greek and commented upon. In this context I will only add that Mithraism knew also about the journey through the seven planetary spheres, this time in reverse order, for in the Mithraic mysteries the journey is not one of descent in which the soul is progressively caught in the webs of the "spheres of necessity," (in other words, it undergoes successive conditionings until it reaches the state of human being), but rather of an ascent which leads one beyond these spheres, in the process of becoming "stripped" of material elements, until one reaches the Ultimate Principle, or the Unconditioned.

The number SEVEN is also found in the initiatory levels of institutionalized Mithraism. These levels were called, in ascending order: Raven (*Corax*); Occult (*Cryphies*); Soldier (*Miles*); Lion (*Leo*); Persian (*Perses*); Sun's Envoy (*Heliodromos*) and Father (*Pater*). According to a common interpretation, a preliminary "mortification" of the inferior nature was required. (This establishes a correspondence with the Hermetic-Alchemical symbolism of the Raven, often associated with the phase called *nigredo*, or the "Work in Black.") After this level, the *miste* enjoys an occult existence (second level). At the third level, he becomes a soldier in the legion of Mithraic initiates, which, according to the war-minded spirit of this tradition, was conceived as a *militia*. The level which followed represented a strengthening of such a quality, while the level of "Persian" emphasized the connection with the origins of Mithraism, namely the ancient Persian cult of Light. As far as the level of *miles* is concerned, Tertullian says that when one person was elevated to it, he was offered a sword and a crown. He would then take the sword, but decline the crown, saying: "My crown is Mithras."

On the level of the Sun's Envoy (the sixth), the initiate reflects the same quality which the myth attributed to Mithras after his confrontation with *Helios*. Finally, the level of *Pater* corresponded to the dignity of a person responsible for initiating others, as well as a leader of a Mithraic community (*pater sacrorum, pater patrum*).

Thus, it appears that if Mithraism had prevailed over Christianity and successfully preserved its central nucleus, the consequence would have been the survival, in the future history of Western civilization, of a regular initiatory Tradition constituted by such nucleus. As far as the external, religious aspect is concerned, Mithras was given the title of *soter* (the Savior, He who Gives Life). It is noteworthy to consider the aspect which had turned the "undefeated God" (*Invictus Mithra*) into the solar patron of the Roman empire; he was considered the giver of the Mazdean *hvareno*, which granted victory, by virtue of a convergence with the ancient Roman tradition of the *Fortuna Regia* (the Latin translation of *tuke basileos*), which expressed itself in the form of that Victory which became the object of a cult in the Roman senate.

Thus, it seems that Mithraism formed a cultural, sacred and initiatory system, which in virtue of its own very nature, could not help but be eliminated during the involutive process which has been affecting the Western world. This involution has gradually removed the West from the horizons of glory and of luminous power, until, at the end, any real contact with the supernatural was irreparably lost. This was indeed a loss despite the survival of an initiation which was no longer the focal point of a system, but only an underground current, enjoying sporadic emergences regardless of the triumph of Christianity.

NOTES

1. I have made a rigorous use of F. Cumont's *Mysteries of Mithras* and *Texts and Bas-Reliefs Relative to Mithras' Mysteries,* as far as the Mithras myth is concerned. When dealing with Mithraic ritual, I have relied upon A. Dieterich's *A Mithraic Liturgy* (Leipzig, 1903) and G.R.S. Mead's *A Mithraic Ritual* (London: TPS, 1907 & Holmes Publishing Group, 1994.).
2. See J. Evola, *L'arco e la clava* (the chapter: "*Il mito di Oriente e Occidente*").
3. In the East, this vital force goes by the name of *tana* (Buddhism); *samsara* (Hinduism); *maya-shakti* (Tantra). In the West, it is known as *Jaldabaot,* taking the name of the "lunar" or "serpentine" principle, the "earthly Venus," the "astral Soul," or the "sidereal Light."
4. A symbolic expression designating those beings who are still *under* the "water," and are dominated by it.
5. All this corresponds to the *preparation* phase, which, by and large, is left up to the initiative of the person to be initiated.

27

6. This is the phase which in Alchemy is called putrefaction, calcination, and mortification. In this phase the "rock" is *dissolved*.

7. It has been rightly observed that initiation is nothing other than the *active* assumption of that process which produces the death of ordinary people. Initiation is the power to induce death, to go through it, in order to re-assert oneself beyond it. Apuleius said that: "Initiation used to be celebrated as a *voluntary death*." (*Metamorphosis*, II, 21).

8. It must be noted that in various initiatory traditions, power, in the strict sense of the word (*shakti* in Hinduism), is conceived of as instrumental passivity, namely as the negative and the feminine element. In relation to the latter, the positive and the masculine element acts as an "unmoved mover," or as one who commands without issuing orders, in virtue of an immaterial initiative and of spiritual determination.

9. Concerning the development of the myth of the fall in relationship to Dyonisius, see Julius Evola, *L'uomo e il divenire del mondo* (Roma, 1926).

10. I have discussed this topic in my books: *La maschera e il volto dello spiritualismo contemporaneo* (at the beginning of the chapter: "*Il neo-misticismo.*"); in *The Doctrine of the Awakening* (the chapter called : "Determination of the Vocations," when denying any relationship between pantheism and Buddha's doctrine); and finally in *L'arco e la clava* (in the chapter "*Il mito di Oriente e Occidente.*"). Concerning the achievement of the supreme and unconditioned state in the Vedantic doctrine, see R. Guenon, *Man and His Becoming in the Doctrine of Vedanta*.

11. The cave in which the "bull" seeks refuge at the end of its run, corresponds to the alchemical "cave of mercury," which is often associated with the subtle center of the body located at the base of the spine, which the Hindu call *muladhara*; the Hindus relate it to the *tattva* of the earth.

12. Emperor Julian, *To the Cynic Heracleios.*, 217C

13. *The Mystery of the Holy Grail and the Ghibelline Imperial Tradition*. Translated by Guido Stucco. Rochester, VT: Inner Traditions, 1996.